BLACKNESS CASTLE

Iain MacIvor

EDITED BY CHRIS TABRAHAM
ILLUSTRATED BY MICHELLE MCCLUSKIE AND DAVE POLLOCK
PHOTOGRAPHY BY HISTORIC SCOTLAND PHOTOGRAPHIC UNIT
DESIGNED BY MAGNUS DESIGN
PRODUCED BY ROY STEWART PRINT SERVICES
PRINTED IN SCOTLAND BY BUCCLEUCH PRINTERS LTD., HAWICK

FIRST PUBLISHED BY HMSO 1982
THIS REVISED EDITION FIRST PUBLISHED BY HISTORIC SCOTLAND 1993
REPRINTED FROM SUSTAINABLE MATERIALS 2004
CROWN COPYRIGHT © HISTORIC SCOTLAND 2003
ISBN 1 903570 11 5

INTRODUCTION

"[Governor Arran] will go to Linlithgow
until his whole force assemble,
and if his enemies come forward
he will remove the Queen
to Blackness, which is impregnable."

(SIR RALPH SADLER IN A LETTER TO KING HENRY VIII OF ENGLAND IN JULY 1543.
WHEN HE WROTE, MARY QUEEN OF SCOTS WAS A CHILD OF SEVEN MONTHS.)

Blackness Castle sits beside the Firth of Forth at the seaport which, in medieval times, served the royal burgh of Linlithgow. The first castle was built in the fifteenth century, by one of Scotland's most powerful families - the Crichtons. But Blackness was not destined to serve as a peaceful lordly residence. In 1453 the castle became a royal castle and its enduring roles were those of garrison fortress and state prison.

In 1537 works started which transformed the castle into one of the most formidable artillery fortifications in Scotland. In 1543, with the building works completed, Blackness Castle received its best known prisoner, Cardinal Beaton of St Andrews. In 1650 the castle was besieged and badly damaged by Cromwell's army but a general repair was begun under King Charles II. The restored fortress was then used to incarcerate Covenanters.

After the Treaty of Union between Scotland and England in 1707 the castle ceased to be used as a state prison and became an obscure minor garrison. During the wars with France between 1759 and 1815, Blackness, like every available space in Crown ownership, was used to hold prisoners of war. In 1870-74 Blackness Castle was converted for use as an ammunition depot. The final chapter in its history came after World War I when the Office of Works removed the depot buildings and conserved the medieval castle as an ancient monument.

Blackness Castle from the air.

THE STORY OF BLACKNESS CASTLE

THE CASTLE OF THE CRICHTONS

The little cove of Blackness is the best natural harbour on the south side of the Firth of Forth west of Queensferry. In the middle ages it was the only feasible position for a seaport to serve the royal burgh of Linlithgow. Ships are mentioned as loading and unloading at Blackness as early as 1200, and its importance increased with the choice of Linlithgow as a principal residence of the royal family.

The arms of the Crichton family.

A castle at Blackness is not, however, mentioned until 1449. At that time the barony was held by the Crichtons, one of the most powerful Scottish families. It seems likely that this first castle was built by Sir George Crichton, Earl of Caithness, Admiral of Scotland, Sheriff of Linlithgow and a cousin of Sir William Crichton, Chancellor to King James II. Nothing is known of Sir George's reasons for choosing to construct a castle at this particular site but it may have been linked to the destruction of his main residence, Barnton Tower on the western outskirts of Edinburgh, by the Earl of Douglas ('the Black Douglas') in the summer of 1444.

From the beginning the plan of Blackness was dictated by the site, a long narrow spit of rock jutting into the Forth. Until the nineteenth century this rock spit was closely surrounded on three sides by sea or salt marsh. In the first building of the 1440s the site was cut off by a rock-cut ditch on the landward side to the south, and enclosed by a defensible wall with a blunt polygonal front towards the south, tapering northward to a point at the tip of the rocky spit. This gives Blackness Castle its unmistakeable resemblance to a ship setting sail into the Forth. Indeed, Blackness is often referred to as "the ship that never sailed".

The defensible wall, called a curtain wall because it was drawn around the rock spit, was not particularly massive and was of modest height when first built. It was topped by a simple parapet with crenellations - openings (called crenels) spaced at intervals to allow the garrison to fire on an approaching enemy but reload their crossbows and long-bows in comparative safety behind the upstanding parts, known as merlons (see the drawing on page 16).

The tower in the centre of the courtyard was probably built at the same time, together with residential accommodation against the curtain walls, including a great hall, or banqueting hall, along the south side. The first historical mention of the castle in 1449 records the castle's use as a state prison, a function which was to continue over two and a half centuries.

Crichton Castle, Midlothian, the ancient seat of the Crichtons: an engraving by R W Billings for his Baronial and Ecclesiastical Antiquities of Scotland (1845-52).

A ROYAL CASTLE

Blackness became a royal castle in 1453 when King James II annexed the lands of Sir George Crichton. It has been Crown property ever since. The castle was placed into the hands of a captain or keeper, who was often also Sheriff of Linlithgow. Its use as a state prison went on, for the most part holding prisoners of high or middle rank in society. The best known prisoner was Cardinal Beaton, Archbishop of St Andrews, who was confined within its walls for about a month in 1543.

Cardinal Beaton, Archbishop of St Andrews 1539-46.

In that same year a building campaign had just been completed which transformed Blackness into one of the most formidable strongholds in Scotland, giving it much of the appearance it has today. This was a time of worsening political relations between Scotland and England. The work was carried out under the direction of Sir James Hamilton of Finnart, one of the most remarkable men of his day. He was the eldest of the nineteen children of the first Earl of Arran (only three of whom were legitimate; James was not among them). Finnart was an exceptional Renaissance Scot: a man of culture, a man capable of great violence, a womaniser, a courtier and a soldier. Most importantly for Blackness, he had an outstanding grasp of military engineering. His own castle at Craignethan Castle in Lanarkshire, built in the 1530s, shows impressive innovation in concepts of defence. In addition to his work at Blackness, Finnart was also Master of Works at Linlithgow Palace and the royal palace in Stirling Castle until his execution on a charge of treason in 1540. The last payment for the works to Blackness were made to the parson of Dysart in Fife in 1542 (clergymen often acted as clerks of works).

The outer gate at Linlithgow Palace, built for King James V by Hamilton of Finnart.

A portrait of King James V, in whose reign (1513-42) Blackness Castle was considerably modified to create a stronghold capable of withstanding the onslaught of heavy guns.
(Courtesy of the National Galleries of Scotland.)

The remodelled Blackness kept to the old plan, but with enormously thickened walls on its most vulnerable east and south fronts and with a generous provision for defensive guns. The strengthened Blackness is of great interest in the story of the development of fortification to take account of the growing threat from artillery. It had none of the subtlety of the elaborate systems worked out in Italy, which were just beginning to penetrate to the rest of Europe: at Blackness a great brute mass of masonry confronted bombardment, with defensive guns positioned to give all-round firepower. Similar ideas of defence had first appeared in Scotland at the blockhouse of Dunbar Castle, completed for the Regent of Scotland some 20 years earlier, and then at Tantallon Castle in a scheme of strengthening undertaken after the siege of 1528.

Modifications seem to have gone on to the 1560s, in the reign of Mary Queen of Scots. The garrison at Blackness held out in support of Mary from the time of her abdication in 1567 until 1573, during which time they harried shipping in the Forth and raided the opposite shores of Fife. The castle was eventually blockaded but not formally besieged, and was in the end taken by a trick.

A fully-pressed siege did not come until 1650, during the conquest of Scotland by Oliver Cromwell's army. The fortress was bombarded by land and sea, with most damage being done by a battery placed on the high ground to the south. When the garrison surrendered, the castle was left in ruins by the English and was not restored until the late 1660s.

GARRISON AND AMMUNITION DEPOT

After the Act of Union of 1707, which brought Scotland and England together as a United Kingdom, Blackness went out of use as a state prison but was kept in repair and occupied by a small garrison. In 1795 there were two gunners, a sergeant, two corporals and about a dozen privates: the posts of governor and deputy-governor were held by non-resident officers as virtually honorary titles.

During the wars with France between 1759 and 1815 the castle, like every other Crown property, was pressed into service to hold some of the 45,000 prisoners of war which the United Kingdom had taken. Blackness mainly acted as a transit camp and occasionally as an overspill prison for Edinburgh Castle, being less secure for large numbers of prisoners.

After the French Wars, the military value of Blackness Castle receded still further and the garrison numbers dwindled until 1870 when it entered the final phase of its active life as a military post - as the central ammunition depot for Scotland. The regiment stationed in Edinburgh Castle provided a garrison for the depot, which lasted barely forty years.

Blackness from the west about 1700, by Captain Theodore Dury, military engineer for Scotland. (Courtesy of the Royal Commission on the Ancient and Historical Monuments of Scotland.)

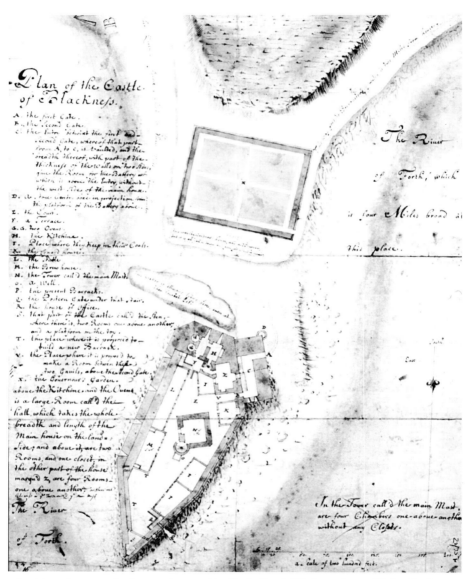

An eighteenth-century plan by an engineer working for the Board of Ordnance (responsible for all military building) giving detailed information on the castle, including the governor's garden.
(Courtesy of the National Library of Scotland.)

THE CASTLE AS ANCIENT MONUMENT

In 1912 the castle was handed over to the Office of Works as an ancient monument. It was reoccupied during World War I and finally abandoned. Between 1926 and 1935 the Office of Works carried out a major programme of conservation and repair. This operation went far beyond what would be expected today, for it swept away the reminders of an unpleasant recent past to return the buildings to a structure more resembling what was perceived to be a medieval castle.

Today, visitors can explore at their leisure the many nooks and crannies and tour the wall-walk of a castle that was in its day one of the strongest places in Scotland.

The castle courtyard in the 1920s. The castle well is just visible in the centre foreground. (Courtesy of the Royal Commission on the Ancient and Historical Monuments of Scotland.)

A Short Tour c

1. Outside the Castle

MOST OF THE BUILDINGS HERE DATE FROM THE 1870-1912 AMMUNITION DEPOT. THE LONGER RANGE ALONG THE SOUTH WAS SOLDIERS' BARRACKS AND THE MORE ELABORATE WEST BLOCK OFFICERS' QUARTERS.

2. Site of Rock-cut Ditch

PROTECTED THE LANDWARD-FACING CURTAIN WALLS. INFILLED IN 1870 WHEN THE GROUND AROUND THE CASTLE WAS LEVELLED TO HOUSE AMMUNITION MAGAZINES.

3. East Curtain Wall

ORIGINALLY FAR THINNER THAN ITS PRESENT THICKNESS OF 5 METRES AND FORMERLY HOUSING THE MAIN ENTRANCE GATEWAY INTO THE CASTLE COURTYARD [6] UNTIL THE PRESENT ENTRANCE WAS OPENED UP THROUGH THE WEST CURTAIN WALL IN MARY QUEEN OF SCOTS' REIGN (1542-67). THE YAWNING GUNHOLES PUNCHED THROUGH THE WALL DATE FROM QUEEN MARY'S TIME ALSO.

4. South Curtain Wall

ONLY HALF ITS PRESENT HEIGHT AND FAR THINNER (1.5 METRES RATHER THAN 5.5 METRES) WHEN FIRST BUILT. THE ORIGINAL CRENELLATED PARAPET CAN BEEN SEEN IMMURED IN THE MASONRY OF THE SOUTH (STERN) TOWER [9] BUILT 1537-43. THE GREAT GUNHOLES AT THE BASE OF THE WALL DATE FROM THEN ALSO.

5. Spur

A HEAVILY-DEFENDED ENTRANCE BUILT DURING QUEEN MARY'S REIGN TO REPLACE THE ORIGINAL ENTRANCE THROUGH THE EAST CURTAIN WALL [3]. ORIGINALLY APPROACHED OVER A DRAWBRIDGE CROSSING THE ROCK-CUT DITCH [2], AND HEIGHTENED IN 1693 TO PROVIDE AN UPPER GUN BATTERY. THE SQUARE EMBRASURES, CRENELLATED PARAPET AND ROUND TURRET DATE FROM THIS TIME. THE IMPRESSIVE WROUGHT-IRON OPEN-BARRED GATE, OR YETT, IN THE OUTER GATEWAY DATES FROM 1693 ALSO.

6. Courtyard

THERE WERE PROBABLY LEAN-TO BUILDINGS AROUND THE COURTYARD FROM THE BEGINNING. ALL REMAINS OF THEM SAVE THE FOUNDATIONS OF THE GUARD-HOUSE WERE REMOVED IN 1870-74 WHEN THE AMMUNITION DEPOT WAS ESTABLISHED AND THE WHOLE COURTYARD SPANNED BY A CONCRETE AND IRON ROOF (SINCE REMOVED). THE COURTYARD BETWEEN 1870 AND 19 WAS ENTERED THROUGH A LARGE OPENING SLAPPEDTHROUGH THE EAST CURTAIN WALL (BLOCKED UP IN THE 1920s). A DRAW-WELL FROM THE MEDIEVAL CASTLE SURVIVES BESIDE THE CENTRAL TOWER [7].

LACKNESS CASTLE

7. CENTRAL [PRISON] TOWER
PROBABLY PART OF THE 15TH-CENTURY CASTLE AND WHICH SEEMS TO HAVE SERVED AS A PRISON FROM AN EARLY DATE. ORIGINALLY WITH THREE STOREYS AND AN ATTIC OVER A VAULTED BASEMENT, BUT HEIGHTENED AND MADE MORE SECURE IN THE 1530s. ALTERED AGAIN IN 1667, WHEN THE STAIR TOWER WAS BUILT, AND USED TO IMPRISON COVENANTERS. AFTER 1707, USED AS BARRACK ACCOMMODATION. EACH APARTMENT HAS A FIREPLACE AND A LATRINE: IT WAS NO COMMON JAIL.

8. NORTH [STEM] TOWER
ORIGINALLY MUCH TALLER BUT REDUCED IN HEIGHT AND CONVERTED INTO A BATTERY FOR THREE GUNS IN 1693. THE TWO REMAINING LOWER STOREYS SERVED AS PRISONS FOR LESS IMPORTANT PEOPLE. THE UPPER CHAMBER HAS A FIREPLACE AND LATRINE AS WELL AS GOOD LIGHT AND VENTILATION. A HATCH IN THE FLOOR GAVE ACCESS TO THE 'PIT', A GRIM HOLE LACKING ALL AMENITIES SAVE THE EBB TIDE 'SLOPPING OUT' TWICE DAILY.

9. SOUTH [STERN] TOWER
PROBABLY THE SITE OF THE GREAT HALL OF THE 15TH-CENTURY CASTLE. THE PRESENT TOWER WAS ADDED 1537-42 AS PART OF THE MAJOR STRENGTHENING OF THE CASTLE DEFENCES AND HOUSED THE PRINCIPAL RESIDENTIAL ACCOMMODATION. IT HAS SINCE BEEN MUCH MODIFIED. THE BUILDING HISTORY OF THE TOWER IS A CONFUSING ONE AND IS BEST EXPLAINED ON PAGES 16 - 19.

10. WATER GATE
A SECONDARY ENTRANCE INTO THE COURTYARD FROM THE SEAWARD SIDE.

11. DRAWBRIDGE AND PIER
BUILT TO SERVICE THE AMMUNITION DEPOT OF 1870-1912 FROM THE FORTH. THE DRAWBRIDGE IS ONE OF THE LAST OF ITS KIND CONSTRUCTED IN BRITAIN.

Artist's bird's-eye view of the castle from the south.

THE DEVELOPMENT OF THE CASTLE

A LORDLY RESIDENCE AND STATE PRISON (1445-1536)

*B*lackness Castle was probably built by Sir George Crichton in the 1440s. From the outset the castle was used not only as a lordly residence but also as a state prison. Indeed, the first historical record in 1449 is in connection with this latter function. At this time, the Crichtons were a political family of the first rank with Sir George's cousin, William Crichton, holding the reigns of power as Chancellor to the youthful King James II and Governor of both Edinburgh and Stirling Castles. The family's positions at the heart of government, together with their personal feuds with the likes of the Black Douglases, would have produced plenty of persons deemed expedient to incarcerate.

Because of the radical changes to the castle's defences carried out after 1537, which had such a profound effect on the residential accommodation, it is very difficult to envisage how the castle was intended to be used throughout its first century of occupation. The main entrance gateway into the castle courtyard was through the east curtain wall (directly opposite the present west entrance). A secondary water gate through the west curtain wall gave access from the seaward side.

An impression of how the castle may have looked from the south in the fifteenth century. The original entrance gateway can be seen in the centre of the east wall.

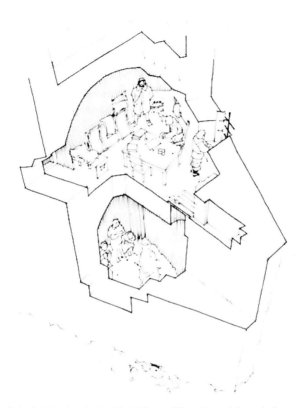

A cut-open sketch of the double prison in the North Tower. Those dropped through the trap-door in the floor of the upper prison must have lost all hope of seeing daylight again.

It is assumed that the main residential accommodation for Sir George Crichton, his family and personal servants (and, after 1453, the keeper and his immediate household) was in the **Central Tower**. Ancillary residential accommodation (for the wider household and guests) and service accommodation (storage cellars, kitchens, bakehouse, brewhouse and stables) were provided in the **North Tower** (subsequently greatly reduced in height) and in lean-to ranges around the courtyard walls. The two bottom storeys in the North Tower were clearly intended as a double prison from the outset. A great hall and chamber block, used for more lavish banquets and for meetings of the barony court, may have stood on the site of the South Tower.

AN IMPREGNABLE FORTRESS (1537-1650)

The Artillery Fortification

In August 1536 Patrick Hepburn, of Waughton Castle in East Lothian, with others was forced to pay a two-instalment penalty of £1000 "*...for the reparacioun and bigging of his* [that is, King James V's] *castell at Blaknes...*" Thus began a major building campaign which continued until the King's death in 1542, and which was completed during the reign of his daughter, Mary. Works were sufficiently completed in 1543 for Blackness to be variously described as 'formidable' and 'impregnable'.

The work begun in 1537 was concentrated at the polygonal south end of the castle, the most vulnerable to a landward bombardment. Large gunholes were punched through the fifteenth-century curtain wall, which was massively thickened internally giving an overall thickness of 5.5 metres. At the same time the whole of the southern part was almost doubled in height to form the present **South Tower**, thereby filling in the fifteenth-century crenellations, which can faintly be seen on the outside face.

With the vulnerable south front greatly strengthened, work was extended to upgrade the curtain walls along the east and west sides. The east curtain wall had further gunholes punched through it before it too was massively thickened. (Both the south and east curtain walls were vulnerable to artillery bombardment from the high ground to the south and south east.)

The opportunity was taken also to relocate the main entrance gateway from the east to the west side of the courtyard. A heavily-defended artillery forework, called the **Spur**, was built against the west curtain wall to protect the new entrance gateway as well as to provide a wing battery to supplement the firepower of the South Tower. The Spur was originally approached by a drawbridge crossing over the rock-cut ditch. Little seems to have been done at this time to strengthen the rest of the west curtain wall or the North Tower.

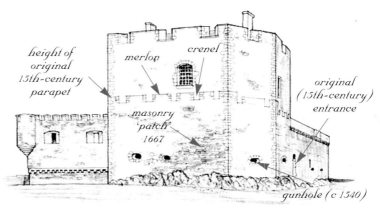

height of original 15th-century parapet

merlon

crenel

original (15th-century) entrance

masonry 'patch' 1667

gunhole (c 1540)

Drawing of the South Tower, emphasising the 'fossilised' fifteenth-century parapet.

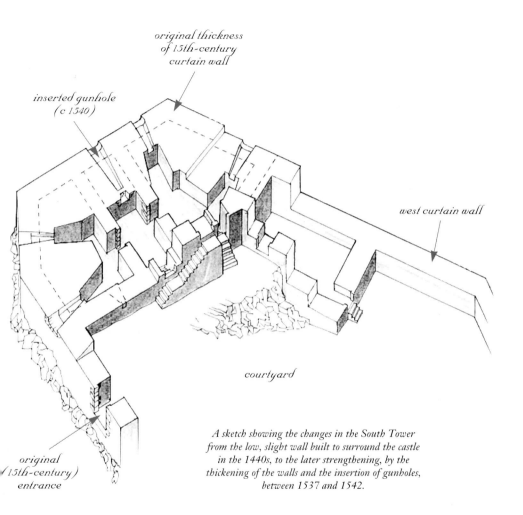

original thickness
of 15th-century
curtain wall

inserted gunhole
(c 1540)

west curtain wall

courtyard

original
(15th-century)
entrance

*A sketch showing the changes in the South Tower
from the low, slight wall built to surround the castle
in the 1440s, to the later strengthening, by the
thickening of the walls and the insertion of gunholes,
between 1537 and 1542.*

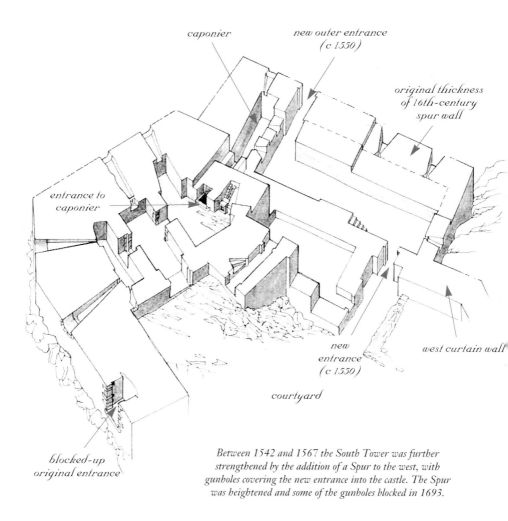

caponier

new outer entrance
(c 1550)

original thickness
of 16th-century
spur wall

entrance to
caponier

new
entrance
(c 1550)

west curtain wall

courtyard

blocked-up
original entrance

Between 1542 and 1567 the South Tower was further
strengthened by the addition of a Spur to the west, with
gunholes covering the new entrance into the castle. The Spur
was heightened and some of the gunholes blocked in 1693.

The Residential Accommodation

The major remodelling of the castle's defences resulted in a reorganisation of the accommodation. The keeper's residence was now in the South Tower and in the wing to its north west. The main apartment, the hall, occupied much of the upper floor in the main block and rose through the full height of the tower. Although much altered in later times, the hall was clearly an impressive space and well suited for dining and entertaining. It had a lofty ceiling (an extra floor was inserted in the seventeenth century but was removed in the 1920s), a large fireplace (later narrowed) in the north wall, and a minstrels' gallery (now gone) which ran the length of the west wall above the door and serving hatch to the kitchen. The hall was not solely for domestic use. The great window in the south wall seems to have been intended from the start to have been capable of serving also as a gun embrasure and still had a gun mounted in it in 1667.

The wing housed additional chambers for the keeper, his immediate family and personal servants. They have also been greatly altered later and scarcely display anything of their sixteenth-century form.

An impression of how the hall in the South Tower may have looked about 1600, with the walls ringing to the sounds of the minstrels and the revellers.

With the principal residential accommodation moving to the South Tower, the Central Tower was converted into more secure prison accommodation. The original attic was removed and a stone vault built in its place. The walls were heightened at the same time, building up from the old parapet which, like the parapet of the South Tower, may be seen 'fossilised' in the later work. The roof may have been used as an exercise yard. This was no ordinary Scottish jail: many of its inmates, mostly political prisoners, were men of rank and consequence and had some degree of comfort in confinement. The three 'cells', one to each floor, each had a fireplace and a latrine closet, and in addition two of them had a further private closet each. It was in the Prison Tower, presumably, that Cardinal Beaton was detained for a month in 1543 before being returned to confinement in his own official residence at St Andrews Castle. In the following year, another distinguished prisoner, Archibald Douglas, sixth Earl of Angus, was incarcerated there.

The lower orders were still expected to be housed in the double prison in the lower storeys of the North Tower (see reconstruction drawing on page 15). The upper prison had at least a fireplace, light and ventilation. The lower 'pit' had nothing to commend it. It was dark, dank and the only facility were two holes through the bases of the walls to let the ebb tide 'slop out' twice a day!

A reconstruction of one of the chambers in the Central (Prison) Tower about 1600, showing its wealthy prisoner enjoying some of the comforts of his station, if not his freedom.

SIEGE AND REPAIR (1650-1707)

Perhaps because of its formidable defences Blackness Castle was not properly besieged until 1650. By now guns were altogether more powerful and Oliver Cromwell's gunfire soon wrought heavy damage on the castle walls forcing the garrison to surrender. Repairs carried out in 1667, using mostly whitish stone, show the extent of the damage. The largest patch partly obliterates one of the gunholes through the south front, by then disused.

    The damage from the English guns brought about alterations and additions both to the defences and to the accommodation. In 1667, the west curtain wall was altered to

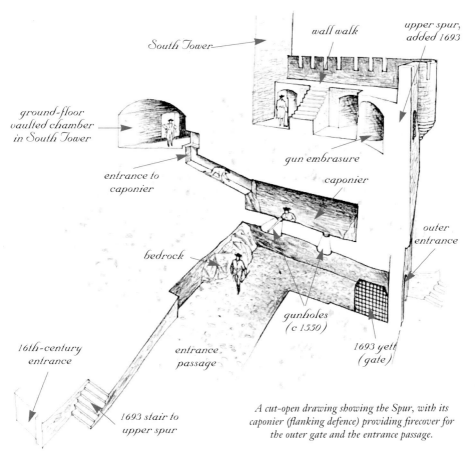

South Tower

wall walk

upper spur, added 1693

ground-floor vaulted chamber in South Tower

gun embrasure

entrance to caponier

caponier

outer entrance

bedrock

gunholes (c 1550)

16th-century entrance

entrance passage

1693 yett (gate)

1693 stair to upper spur

A cut-open drawing showing the Spur, with its caponier (flanking defence) providing firecover for the outer gate and the entrance passage.

The yett (iron gate) at the outer entrance gateway, carefully overlooked by a gunhole.

its present width and height, whilst in the South Tower the ground-level gun emplacements were abandoned and blocked while part of this level was converted into the castle bakehouse. (The ovens were removed and the gunholes opened out in the 1920s.) The upper storeys of the South Tower were remodelled also. A stair tower, between the main block of the tower and its wing, gave better access to these upper floors. The original height of the hall was reduced by the insertion of an extra floor (since removed), and the suite of rooms in the wing, opening from the hall, represents a complete replanning of the medieval arrangement. At the same time the Central Tower was altered when the projecting stair-tower was built.

In 1693 further work was carried out to improve the defences. The Spur was radically altered, raised in height and given an upper gun battery and wall-walk facing south and west. The square embrasures, the crenellated parapet and the round turret date from this time, as does the large wrought-iron yett or gate in the outer entrance gateway.

In the same year the North Tower was reduced in height and platforms provided for three heavy guns covering the seaward side.

The castle from the north east. The stunted North (Stem) Tower on the right originally stood much higher until it was reduced in 1693 to provide a better gun battery.

A MILITARY DEPOT (1707-1912)

After the Treaty of Union in 1707 created a United Kingdom, Blackness Castle ceased to be a state prison and settled into a life as a minor garrison. The garrison's task was to maintain and man the artillery guns. To complement the accommodation in the South Tower, the Central Tower was adapted as soldiers' barracks. Each of the three rooms provided space for perhaps eight men sleeping two to a bed. They drew their rations daily from the castle stores but cooked and ate their meals in their rooms.

The quiet tedium of garrison life was rudely interrupted during the French Wars between 1759 and 1815 when Blackness Castle served as a prison of war, usually for prisoners in transit to and from Edinburgh Castle. There is no evidence of works being carried out to receive them.

The decision in 1870 to make Blackness Castle the new central ammunition depot for Scotland brought about a great change to the castle's fabric. Between 1870 and 1874 the War Office altered the superstructure of the three towers, covered in the whole of the courtyard with a concrete and iron roof, placed a water tank in the infilled rock-cut ditch, levelled an area east of the castle as a site for ammunition magazines, built new barracks with other garrison accommodation, and constructed a cast-iron pier out into the Forth from the castle.

After World War I the castle was finally abandoned as a military depot and the new body responsible for the fabric, the Office of Works, undertook to 'restore' the medieval castle. Between 1926 and 1935 they demolished most of the late-Victorian works, the only structures to survive the operation being the barracks to the south of the castle, the water tank in the ditch and the drawbridge and pier. The courtyard roof was removed and the upper parts of the towers were rebuilt to something resembling their ancient form.

The river front from the west about 1920 showing the drawbridge and pier in working order.

FURTHER PLACES TO VISIT

Blackness Castle is one of a number of ancient monuments in Historic Scotland's care associated with the Crichton family and with James Hamilton of Finnart.

CRICHTON CASTLE (2 miles west of Pathhead in Midlothian)
The ancient seat of the Crichtons, and the home of Chancellor Crichton, the cousin of Sir George Crichton of Blackness. A very fine medieval castle with architecture spanning the 14th to the 17th century.

LINLITHGOW PALACE (4 miles inland from Blackness)
A splendid royal palace displaying the finest architecture of the Stewart kings and queens. The crowning glories were added under the eye of Sir James Hamilton of Finnart for King James V.

CRAIGNETHAN CASTLE (8 miles south of Hamilton in Lanarkshire)
A formidable castle built by Finnart in the 1530s for his own use. It displays all the finesse and accomplishment of an architect and military engineer with the freedom to build on a green-field site, rather than having to modify an existing and somewhat antiquated fortress.

STIRLING CASTLE (In Stirling)
Although the documentation does not come together easily to give a clear story, it is certain that Finnart built the magnificent Renaissance palace in Stirling Castle for James V before he fell from royal favour and was executed in 1540 before work was finished.

FURTHER READING

ON THE CASTLE:

D MacGibbon & T Ross *The Castellated and Domestic Architecture of Scotland*, vol 3 (1889)

I MacIvor 'Artillery and Major Places of Strength in the Lothians and East Borders, 1513-42' in D Caldwell (ed) *Scottish Weapons and Fortifications 1100-1800* (1981)

C McWilliam *The Buildings of Scotland: Lothian* (1978)

Royal Commission on the Ancient and Historical Monuments of Scotland *Inventory of Midlothian and West Lothian* (1926)

ON OTHER LINKED CASTLES:

S Cruden *The Scottish Castle* (1981)

I MacIvor *Craignethan Castle* (1993)

C Tabraham *Scottish Castles and Fortifications* (1990)

C Tabraham *Scotland's Castles* (1997)

ON THE HISTORICAL BACKGROUND:

G Donaldson *Scotland: James V - James VII* (1971)

R Nicholson *Scotland: The Later Middle Ages* (1974)

C McKean 'Hamilton of Finnart', *History Today*, vol 43 (1993)